Riddles, Etc.

Geoffrey Hilsabeck

The Song Cave

Published by The Song Cave
www.the-song-cave.com

Cover image: © 2002 Claes Oldenburg and Coosje van Bruggen, *Soft Viola*, 2002. Photograph by Ellen Page Wilson

Design and layout by Janet Evans-Scanlon

ISBN: 978-0-9988290-1-2
Library of Congress Control Number: TK

FIRST EDITION

for my teachers

That which is, is far off, and deep, very deep;
who can find it out?

—ECCLESIASTES

Table of Contents

Today a Casual Essay, Tomorrow a Love Letter

I've never seen the Ohio River.
I slept as we crossed it on horseback and by car.
They say it is made of steel
as a schoolteacher is and fire
as are her students
but it seems to me it is made mostly of water.
The Ohio River reminds me of water
its ready availability
how it goes hot and cold, room temperature
how it becomes the room and the shore.
Please. We have to admire at least that about it.
We have to admire the Ohio River
even as we pity its lack of knowledge
and we pity its single-mindedness:
for it isn't the Hudson going first this way then that.
Or is it?
I don't know. Like I said, I've never seen the Ohio River.

But I know it flows through fields and pipes
and wildflowers seen from the road
or on an afternoon walk
but the river can't feed the walker
dumb, purposeful, like an elephant
it continues its steady march a man on its back

not even pausing to admire his hunger, rich as caves
and able, if pressed, at a certain hour in a certain light
to send out flocks of deadly black bats
like letters of different colors, different stinks
different bone structure—
to read those different letters—
please, we have to be in awe of, as it were,
    the bone structure of those letters.
We have to wonder at the hunger of the walker.
How it hollows him out, leaves just a brush of flame.
Gaping yawn of his hunger
empty house of his hunger
empty open night:
no one cries, or only a few. A few cry.

I was moved today to speak up for the Ohio River
though, as I said, I've never seen it.
But that hardly matters.
It is not the river I speak of
not the river that moves me
as a dog is moved to shift positions
to get up from its corner of the kitchen
and move to its corner of the living room
with a *harrumph* and a sigh
as a dog is drawn to the wounded
it is what was drawn to the river that draws me.

A Love Letter

Let me walk with you a ways. Let me, can I, look at you, laughing. Shy with you. Let me ask you something, catch only a few phrases, new phrases to mull over and wear. Things touched and seen, the slippery ginger of dreams. Let me, laughing, lie with you, call you flower, rub your color between two fingers.

Riddle 1

It's raining sulfuric acid on Venus
Saturn is a chilly 270° below

At the far end of the eyehole
Jupiter stares blankly back at you
oceans of eddying gas and endless lightning storms

Dear citizen stargazer
what am I
I scoot by even water can't hold me
I slip from its grip pass on

Empty me of significance and you discover
why I matter
why anything does for that matter

Breathing and moving
my form fits its purpose perfectly
this finite constellation of fins and gills
cosmos incarnate matter articulate

I am you are the waters are held
by gravity's hands the sun is the king of the system

Refuge

Thank you grass
for the grass
which says what it knows and nothing more

Every morning the moon drowns
You bear witness standing there
a drop of water in your hand

Riddle 2

Think of shrouds
sheeting matter from matter

or if you'd rather two ships at sea
the fat captain and his first mate
two deckhands a cook lots of wine
a rocky crossing

Oyster shells with their watery cargo

Imagine a shepherd tending his small flock
and across the valley another

Shadows a pair of them
slipped on to go out
dark clouds to settle into

Lay down again among murderers
then get up and put these on

Ruy Belo

I have been translating from Portuguese a poet
who as a young man before he left
the Church belonged to Opus Dei.
He studied canonical law in Rome.
I never get his name right.
But he left and he wondered
what happened to childhood and spilled
the animal spirit of the sad, an animal sadness,
olive trees in rain men working
things all the things left to themselves
sunset being nothing and nobody else
across a thousand pages, more, drew from stones
the music necessary to continue.
I cannot get his rhymes right
these casual quatrains on the death
of a famous cyclist, day dying,
how he kills himself by letting both arms fall,
a minha maneira de me matar
é deixar cair ambos os braços.
I want to translate "Humphrey Bogart"
but can't get it right. Pure-water gaze.
The poet's brother. Only sunset
sunset only sunset and not even sunset.

Riddle 3

I am flat and cannot be gathered.
The earth is not mine, neither are the rivers.

This flickering existence—
as Wakefield walked next to his own life

looking in on it now and then and smiling
I walk next to mine.

No. 9 Baladeuse

He bathes
a wet rag and then a lily dried
and tied in a string.

I have to write a letter to nobody
not even you with summer
another word for pleasure
moths for ships
Demoiselle or Grasshopper
pale grey to green
with bamboo limbs, strings
of piano wire for warping.
The wings are made of paper.
Below, hills like strange
casements, crepe-paper poppies
flourishing biography
the flourishing of biography.
At night when strips of rubber
cover the sky harp-hands
calloused as light as gesture
turn blunt like shovels.

Ruin in her rickety chariot rattled the rabbit warren.
Again her racket-Iscariot battles and habits war then.
Then stacks her lariats riots of metal crab of arson.
Raining sporadic *tsk*s with air idiot-mottled and rabid, soon
rain against laughter or aria. Lions dead in drab pits, dens.
Planes against laughter. Ariel unsaid. Instead enraptured men
ruined on scabbed, upturned land, burial. Read. Wrap. Inter. Mend.

Knots: lark's head, toggle and tiller hitch,
surgeon's and half-blood knot, round turn, bowline,
double sheet

Flowers: dandelions for the common, dirty, much-maligned, and
tulips for Europe, double peonies, day-lilies,
irises for melancholy,
carnations because they're cheap,
wildflowers without names and because you scatter their seeds

Burials: by land or the hand of fire

Riddle 4

No color no taste
neither crooked nor straight
it cannot be counted
amounting to a motion oceanic
a way to measure my days

Harder to hold than water
fleeter and meaner than earth
empty and temperamental
does it come and go as it pleases
or is it too the servant of some master?

Nothing in itself
idle and excess and strange
it is what remained
after lighting the stars
setting the grass growing

Do you have a metaphysics?
You have to have a metaphysics
Mine goes
No color no taste
neither crooked nor straight

Riddle 5

I moult
and moult
and moult
then emerge
to gather flags
and figure
wind
but oh!
how hard
it is
to be handled
by wind

After Carlos Drummond de Andrade

In the middle of my throat there is a stone
there is a stone in the middle of my throat
there is a stone
in the middle of my throat there is a stone

Like the Rat Man I lift it
out of the way then put it back
worn out by the fact that on the open road of my throat
there is a stone
there is a stone in the dark wood of my throat
in the green well of my throat there is a stone

Waltish

Past the gate through that
rough hole
flows the waste
of a hidden world

My body too lightly touched
in the transit of glances
my nervous working body of twos
two hands two knees testicles elbows earlobes

This old ark
hulled in Europe
harpsichorded and bouqueted there
this drifting toward shore

toward an Indian graveyard
fetish of grave names

Alaska

There was not night there were dogs
in a wire pen
grouse in black spruce, moose, grizzlies
nuzzling the dump

There was a cannery a jail an inn
and in the inn a jailed Indian
singing

Caribou ambling north
winter making its way through the woods
stripping the trees of their jewels

There was no day
fishing boats bumping in the harbor
a sky made violent by stars

At the bar I watched a woman dance
stomping around the waxed plywood floor
black hair to her waist
back-and-forth hair of hexes and exes
a black axe to cut my throat

Riddle 6

This thing's dirty as money as fun to clutch
an empire for an emperor to survey

Call it an eon-in-an-instant
the fire thing then the closed smoke of composure

as if a heart split
as if a heart could split

It's as gray as a newspaper
as full of music

When I'm busy about the rooms
it's secret portable

Here is my oyster cracking her water grin
Here is my olive Rosalind

My shelter my bread here is the table
The crowd is dispersed

the cages closed and locked
It's an empire for an emperor

The facility is sanitary
An air conditioner is in the room

See Volume II and Volume III for additional information
The cage is thrown open the body dragged out

restrained stripped secured with Mylar
torn through the screaming darkness

When one of the guards raised an eyebrow
he would walk to the water table

When one of them snapped his fingers
he would lie down on it

Here is the desk the papers the lamp
Here is my hand holding the answer

I take its pulse nope
listen for a heartbeat it's heartless

It's the thing that killed the clumsy giant
God's thing for God's king

the blood moon summoning more soldiers
the jailer moon above the books at Calais

Here is the book it says love
what's approaching preserve your independence

your childish insistence on certain facts
the dignity of all things even this

From the Tether of My Position

in my muted human way of rage
I consider dimensions
I take care to consider each element
every facet of the problem
its symmetries and mysteries
its repetitions
sense of the infinite about it
the eye that black city by the sea
what white horizons
the comportment of the forehead
the ears off to the side out of the way
my ears are gutters gathering rain
butter on my lips
lower still these silly spidering legs
these ankles wet with testament
the witness part of me as well
Is this the body that wrote the psalms
wrote angrily to the musicians
to God wrote its incomplete complaints?

Partial

I was on my knees again
in the dark in the dark
was called went

All the clothes in all the closets were restless

I buried myself
up to the nose and held myself in my hand

Thank you if you did that for me

Riddle 7

Traveler, head like a spade, an inch, two?
Its body in three pieces, three drops of ink
forever walking across five continents.
It scuttles on six legs. It tarries
strategically. O apt carapace.
Not embodied but encased it doesn't breathe it's breathed
like a tiny recorder seven holes
for seven fingers but whose fingers?
For how long?

Holy City

Today is Wednesday
something cold in it something warmer and errant
later a cart

a stranger in it
haunting the side of a house roaming
at evening then entering.

Today is like something stolen
something heavy in its own hands
today loosed on tomorrow

a mess of crickets scrubbing their wings
with their wings.
Around the songpost a long string winds.

The Bones of Thoreau

I sleep on a rubber bed
wake up in the dark
music above music below
the crowded seat of my still body.

There is a feeling that grows
from a feeling very adult that way
an unhappy business
of the crooked and lacking

the narrow and mean.
This poem rejects the values
of the New York Times
pity shame contemplation.

Sappho says sweetbitter the uprising
Eros inside me. Eros once again
addressing my neighbors
I hate you. I hate you more

than your husband I hate him more than his children
I hate them more than their dog
dust and snow in its paws bloody nose
nuzzling muzzle of animal night.

My neighbors from Nantucket New Canaan Carlisle
their shared store of winters and in the cemeteries
so many moldering historically important
human bones the bones

of the animals floating from the Concord
to the Merrimack and from there.
I wake up in the afterlife walk out into it.
Not the soldier's or the scholar's world

a squash-on-Sundays world, a weekends-in-Maine-
two-weeks-on-the-Vineyard-in-August's world
skin drawn close across the bones
of my neighbors made of clapboard and brick.

Their Maine their August my knuckle my tongue
luxury commodities
formed from the slurry of futures
and the interest on a derivative.

Riddle 8

The tower has fallen
The people have scattered
Even the dead are on the move

This thing stays put
It conducts its business from bed

I ask it about myself
It doesn't answer
It's busy holding up the world

I shake it *hey I'm talking to you*
shout *Red Oak Black Oak Cork Bur Sessile*
It doesn't respond
stubborn and yielding stock-still and shivering
heavy at the base all light and flight up high
half air up there

I grab my hammer and saw and get to work
making ships and crosses shingle palaces
and shingle cities
I loose the ghost of carbon from its cage

Somewhere up in the leafy reaches
God buries his head in his hands
He laughs in disbelief

Riddle 9

Once it was a fist.
Later it opened
and from its quiver
five arrows shot out
to infinity.

Anaxagoras
thought man the wisest
animal because
he had these. Two hounds
up with you at dawn
always at your side.
Or emissaries
from reality.

I like how they pet
pat and put themselves
in pockets. What's mine?
Nothing Yours? *Nothing*

Bottom of July

I have traveled worked studied
covered and uncovered encountered
the hard bars of what won't be
with my fists and mouth my teeth even.
And it's like it can't be handled.
I have drifted and landed
become mammalian
how mammals nuzzle that's how I do too.
My train now has a sleeper car.
The grass is a lawn I sometimes attend to.
And people look good. They look like stars
caught doing something so everyday
pushing, carrying, day shaking from its hair
flakes of something soft
and percussive. Folk plucks.
I am bent in it peering
my fingers in it
my body absurd stubborn and shy.
I take my body somewhere
day still strapped to the land
the sky in pieces
white scraps out of the east
settling into the soft forms
that snow takes. My odd body

its want of finish the like in it
that finds likeness elsewhere.
In the parking lot
the Christians are enjoying their gelato.
The dark grubby places in rocks faint stink
on my fingertips
little desperate bud of what?

Riddle 10

I clean them, clip their
crowns. Old dumb giants
with a few black hairs.

Bare mechanicals.
They know so little
of the earth, other

animals even.
Odd duck and odd duck:
flat like that. Protube-

rances with protube-
rances, potatoes
with bones. Root cellars.

Send my roots rain Lord
send my dogs water
old giants new lands

and to animals
other animals
and to me Lord days

send days and nights without end.

Riddle 11

You don't ask me to read Homer and Shakespeare with you. You leave me like an overcoat as you pass through elegant galleries considering the clean lines of Mondrian, Byzantine glitter, etc. I know nothing of the stars or the bottom of the ocean. I like to poke around bushes and float through the air like a big, fat bee in search of sugar. No one, or only the truly perverse, would call me beautiful, but I'm not sure why, for I can be shapely like a thigh, as delicate as fingers. You look right past me. I belong to a less civilized time, when space squatted so close to the earth it smelled like a struck match.

Riddle 12

A book without pages
twenty stories each one just the same

Twenty servants in a paper house
summon one he rushes up
wavers like he's been drinking
then settles
the faithful retainer on fire with tasks

Folding in on itself like a bug
like a thing with wings

I have hundreds of half-finished poems
but never one of these when I need it
in a drawer somewhere or stuffed
in a coat pocket
to scratch a little ceremony
into an otherwise ordinary evening

In a Room Called Days

I left the city on foot alone.
It was a Friday in May
hours before my birthday.
The road was level and bare and free of trees
ditches littered with milky algae.
The lark accompanied me
for some way and then went home.

At midnight I saw my old city
black canal coursing through its body
and at noon a green cricket emerged
from a drawing of feathers.
Midnight my hand was trawling the water.
Noon I was breathing but dimly, fleetingly
as a moth might be.

The teeth of the woods are scored with laws.
Don't wash in milk don't talk to the dead.
Fix your eyes on what's holy what glows.
Hiding in the bread pretending it's smoke. Hang
broken things from whole things. Break the bread
in two. Listen. Nothing is singing.

Riddle 13

I am loose like a gas, common as water.
We are three ways of saying the same thing.

No lower. I come after, always. I am, like you,
the substance of time. Everywhere earth stuff

every color once the colors have gone,
every object and article, all items,

I am what bodies were and will be
having passed through the fires of a life.

Notebook

Less than twenty, light and white as a candle,
my childhood pooling like wax at my feet,
I wandered through aisles hemmed-in like rail lines
along a river—the mystic Hudson—
towering stacks of books on either side
of me, a catacomb or a garden,
and look! a carnation in the garden:
red, cheap, largely incomprehensible
but lush with relationships, heavy with life,
water and light, the footprints of visitors.
I plucked it and stuck it in my pocket.
Outside, New York humming, New York sprawling
with human chances, my life, that secret act,
becoming strange and unnecessary.

Remaking the Music Box

First unhurt the accidents.
Plant yourself in what remains
dressed in bright colors a brightly colored urn.
Hear a frequency distant, spectral.

Lay down newspaper
(like the roses covering your bones)
and drag your palm across the surface
as if it were a horse's heaving flank.

Be proud, disagreeable, hidden, joyful, bewildered:
you'll need a Kent
to carry your rainbow, a Fool to insist that a
rainbow is just a rusty parabola.

No sadness just disaster
no meanness just thrift.
Out of nothing something and out of something
nothing: all in a day's work.

Riddle 14

Gravity and levity coexist in me.

Riddle 15

It's more like an Elizabethan air
than Bede's death song or Caedmon's hymn.
Poor Caedmon was alone when a man came
saying sing to me the beginning of things
and Caedmon praised what was made
the sky first and then the earth.
This thing though keeps company.
It comes in infinite variations
the same themes finding multiple expressions.

It went from solid to gas
then gas through a coil became liquid
resurrected a burned water and sacred
dressed up in the aroma of flora
and the quickness of citrus and served
with a rinse and a twist on the rocks or not.
A *frisson* a *jouissance* a *dérangement.*
Put a lit match in your mouth and breathe.
It's a wellspring watering everything.

Brackish, Lean, Blazing

Strange cold stones are taking place
here particular, elsewhere particular.

Riddle 16

This fat thing
hops around on matchsticks
scratching out its hours
on the red dirt floor of its house.
It's an orderly life.
The door slides open in the morning
night comes the door closes.
This feathered, long-fingered thing
flutters and then stays put
utterly thiswordly.

Another Love Letter

When you call me my something somethings. A night so cold it froze to the bottom of the canoe melts into noon. Together we discover each other there, highly everyday animals having approximations. Our hands so many handsome uses for them. Our legs like the first musical. Our eyes that see so much, can do so little—that give us away. Outside the window two moths chase each other across the street. They bounce and carom off invisible walls. Such lightness to the task and everything at stake.

Riddle in Two Parts 17

I

I am not I not really.
It's useful to say so though.
Think of me like a door slowly opening
black wind whistling in from another vaster world
a world without edges
hardly a world at all.

I am not anything not really
the breaking of the golden bowl
the settling in of birds to their feathers
their fragile houses.
The hour arrives.
The orchestra takes its seats.

II

I talk first quietly then loudly
my voice rising as things rise in me
and things rise in themselves too
they rise up to meet themselves.
But enough about rising.

Am I a stone fence, a cold gavel?
Neither. No, more like
a bucket of water dumped onto the street
or better
a coat of paint scraped away
to show the original beneath
interior, landscape, portrait.

Not to this or that to this and that
to each this and to every green that
I return
open and plain utterly candid
for I am fearfully, wonderfully made.

Sleeves, Smoke

He went south in search of something he saw
sleeves at the elbow, smoke as an instrument.

Little green, red, and blue boats, snug as shoes.
South. Buys his flowers from a grocer.

Shoes: his simple mission to honor the life
of things. Hard bench of life, sit on it.

His brother will be buried beside him.
How he talks and jaws to the dead stars.

Paints sunflowers for Paul, hangs them, waits—
great multicolored crowds of life, corners here

and there unfinished, reworkings, roughnesses:
he went and the stars in search of something

bury themselves beside him. Their jaws.
No system, shoes at the elbow and under the sleeves, smoke.

Hard bench of life, nails in it, nails on the wall
where pictures hung, nails in the shoes of the poor.

Where the stars jaws shoes systems become smoke
he waits but it runs from him

that high yellow note, genius of the French geographers,
so rare as to seem a mistake

so free it reminds him of flowers, or boats in a tub.
Sit on the edge of the tub, honor the little boats.

He went south in search of something he saw.
He found there a way to talk about flowers

and boats and stars. Used instruments.
Little green, red, and blue instruments.

This tale reminds me of my brother.
Boats in a tub. Friendship, that free form

of relation, a simple and poor geography, done
in the rough style of if you get there first, wait.

Notes and Acknowledgments

"Ruy Belo": Ruy Belo was a midcentury Portuguese poet. The italicized lines come from his poem "Tristeza Branda."

"No. 9 Baladeuse": The title of this poem refers to the smallest of 21 airships designed by the pioneering Brazilian aviator and engineer Alberto Santos-Dumont in 1903. As a young man, Santos-Dumont could be seen tooling around Paris in No. 9, a kind of floating opera box. Years later, broken, in part, by the uses to which his airships had been put in World War I, Santos-Dumont hanged himself with his necktie at a hotel in his native Brazil.

Riddle (6) makes use of some sentences from the executive summary of the Senate Select Committee on Intelligence's report on the C.I.A.'s use of torture.

"Remaking the Music Box": The first line of the last stanza is something Jasper Johns once said.

"Sleeves, Smoke" takes some of its language from the letters of Vincent Van Gogh.

The poems in this book owe their existence to many people besides myself, some of whom I want to thank here on their behalf: Elizabeth Gramm, Burke Hilsabeck, Steve and Alison Hilsabeck, Paul Kane, Mark Levine, Amanda Nadelberg, Cecily Parks, Chicu Reddy, Debbie Rogow and Howie Winant, Miguel Tamen. Thank you to the editors of the following journals in which these poems first appeared, sometimes in altered form: *6x6, Seneca Review*, and *WE ARE SO HAPPY TO KNOW SOMETHING 3*. Thank you, especially, to Ben and Alan at Song Cave for all their work on this book. And thank you, always, to Johanna.

Answers to the Riddles

1 Fish

2 Shoes

3 Shadow

4 Wind

5 Dragonfly

6 Stone

7 Ant

8 Tree

9 Hands

10 Feet

11 Nose

12 Matchbook

13 Dust

14 Bird

15 Cocktail

16 Chicken

17 Night and Day

OTHER TITLES FROM THE SONG CAVE:

1. *A Dark Dreambox of Another Kind* by **Alfred Starr Hamilton**
2. *My Enemies* by **Jane Gregory**
3. *Rude Woods* by **Nate Klug**
4. *Georges Braque and Others* by **Trevor Winkfield**
5. *The Living Method* by **Sara Nicholson**
6. *Splash State* by **Todd Colby**
7. *Essay Stanzas* by **Thomas Meyer**
8. *Illustrated Games of Patience* by **Ben Estes**
9. *Dark Green* by **Emily Hunt**
10. *Honest James* by **Christian Schlegel**
11. *M* by **Hannah Brooks-Motl**
12. *What the Lyric Is* by **Sara Nicholson**
13. *The Hermit* by **Lucy Ives**
14. *The Orchid Stories* by **Kenward Elmslie**
15. *Do Not Be a Gentleman When You Say Goodnight* by **Mitch Sisskind**
16. *HAIRDO* by **Rachel B. Glaser**
17. *Motor Maids across the Continent* by **Ron Padgett**
18. *Songs for Schizoid Siblings* by **Lionel Ziprin**
19. *Professionals of Hope* by **Subcomandante Marcos**
20. *Fort Not* by **Emily Skillings**